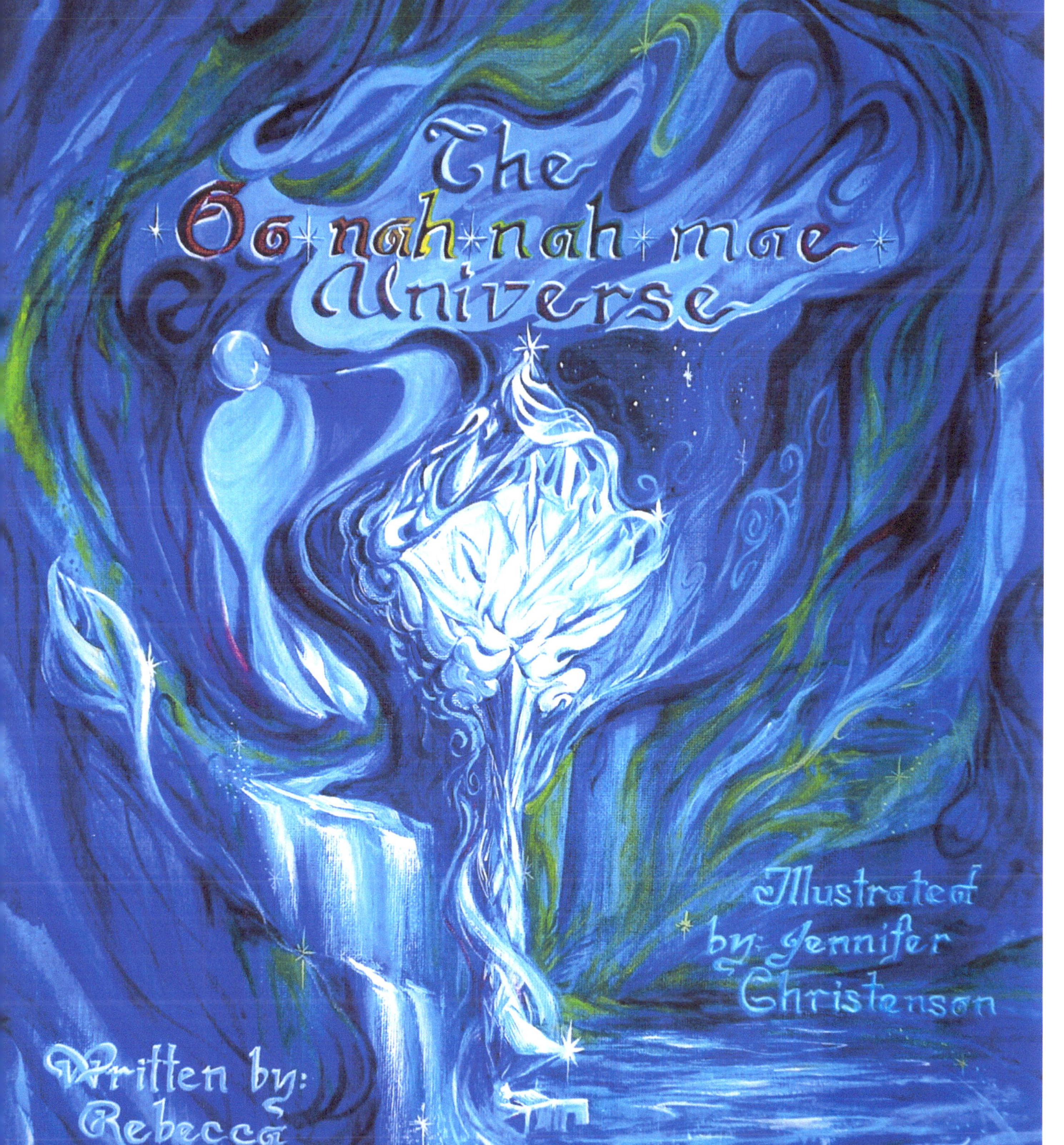

The
Go·nah·nah·mae
Universe
Illustrated
by: Jennifer
Christenson
Written by:
Rebecca
Christenson
2011
J. Christenson

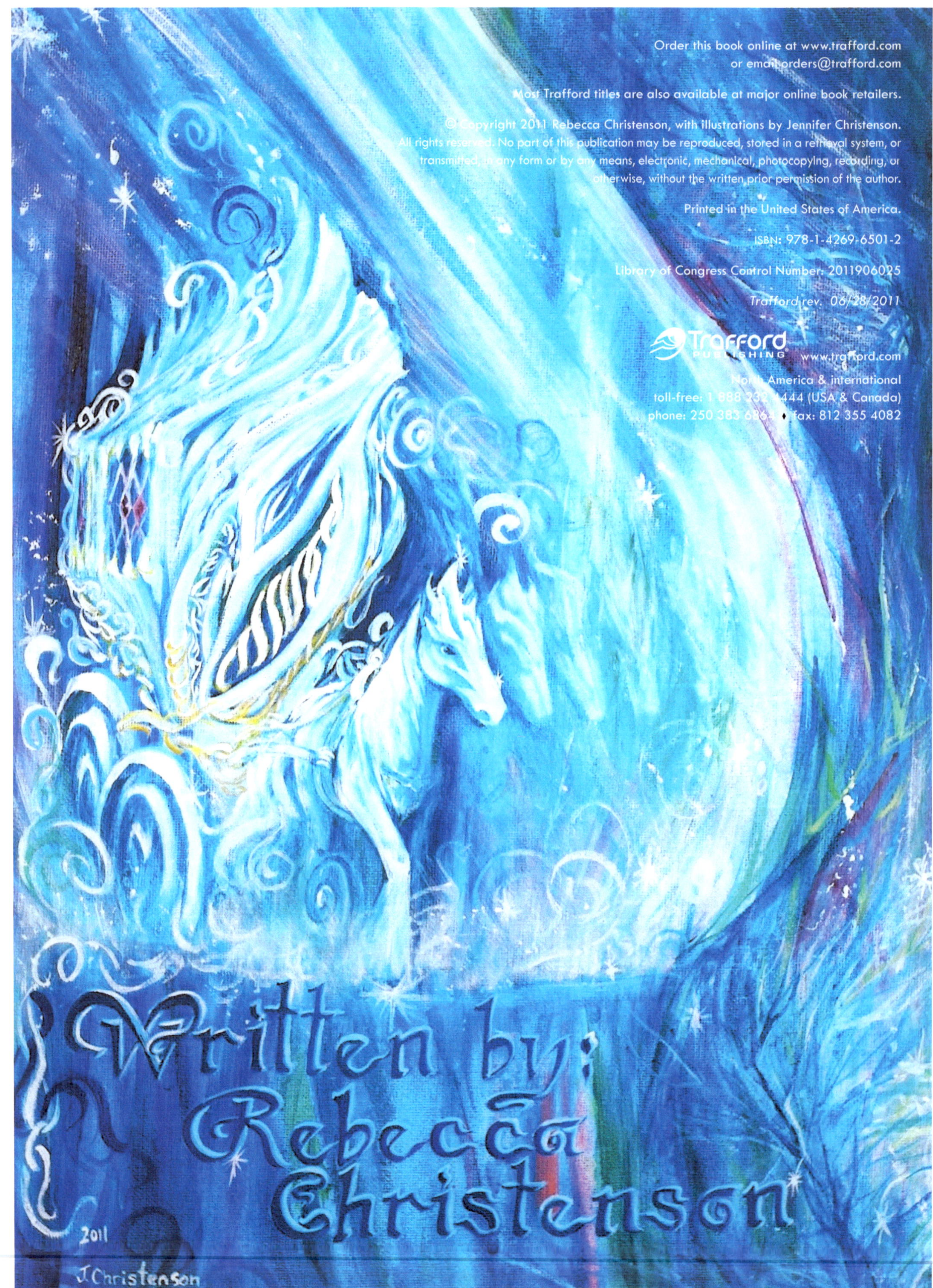


Order this book online at www.trafford.com
or email orders@trafford.com

Most Trafford titles are also available at major online book retailers.



Printed in the United States of America.

ISBN: 978-1-4269-6501-2

Library of Congress Control Number: 2011906025

Trafford rev. 06/28/2011

Trafford PUBLISHING www.trafford.com
North America & international
toll-free: 1 888 232 4444 (USA & Canada)
phone: 250 383 6864 • fax: 812 355 4082

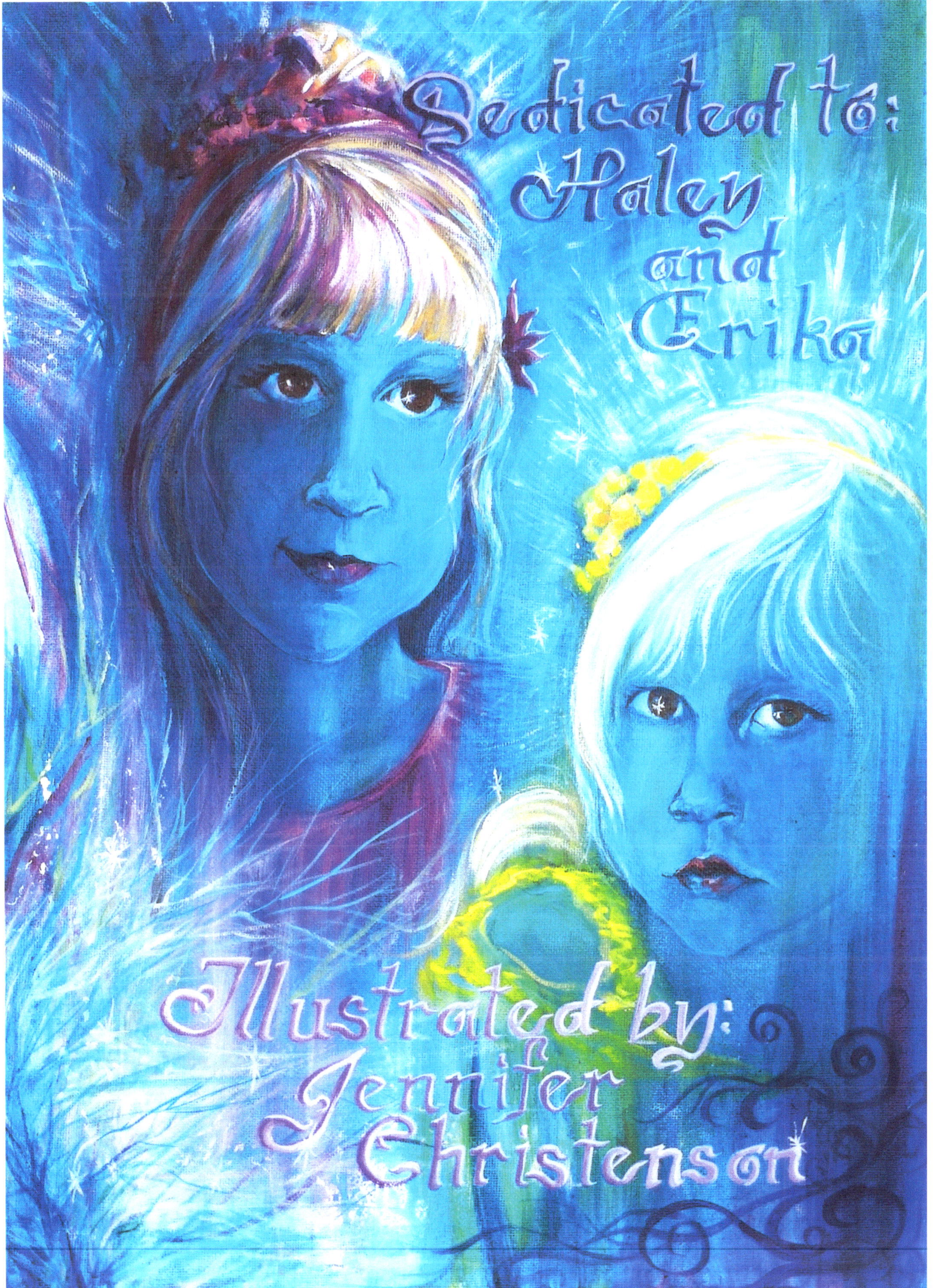
Dedicated to:
Haley
and
Erika
Illustrated by:
Jennifer
Christenson

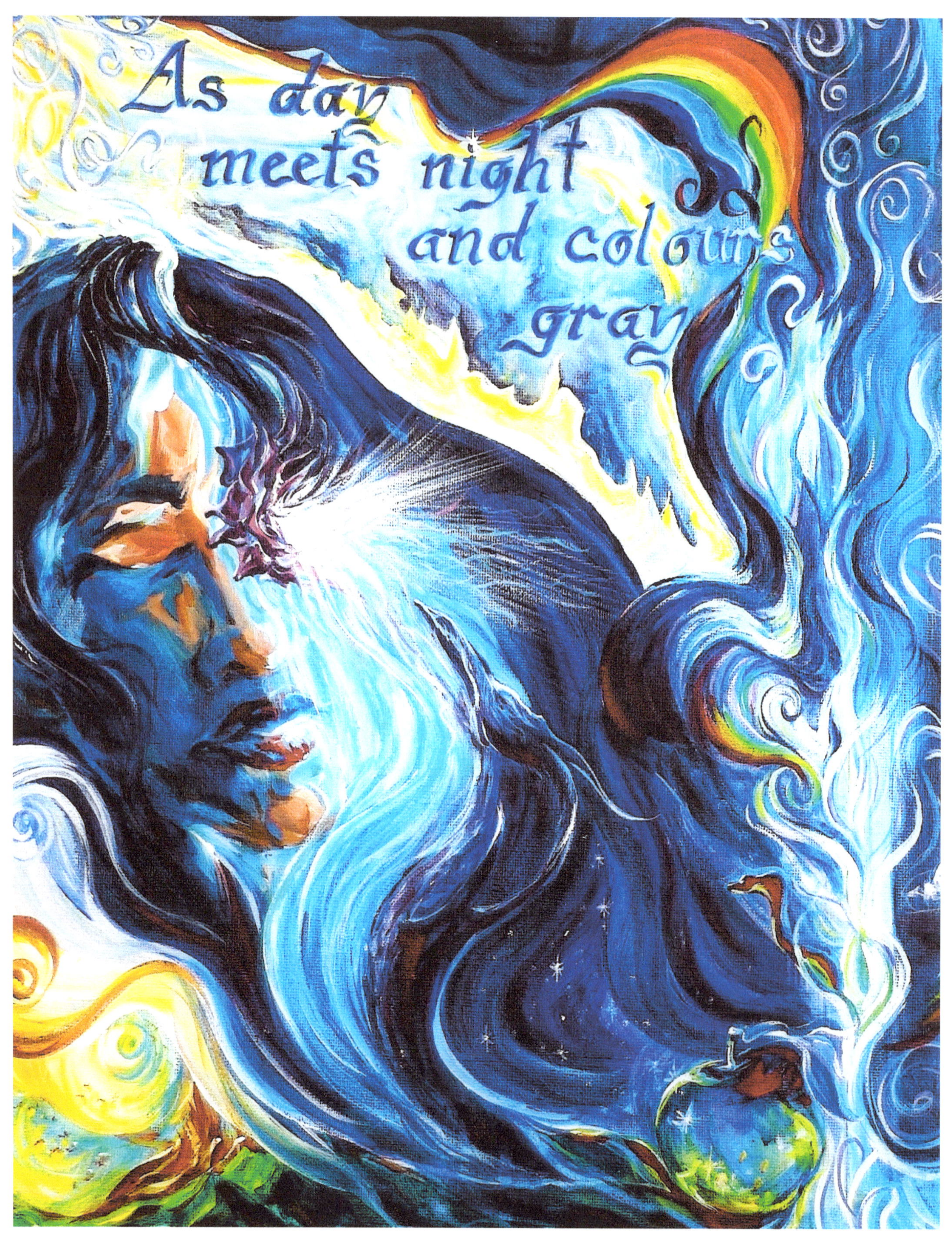


*As day meets night and colors gray*

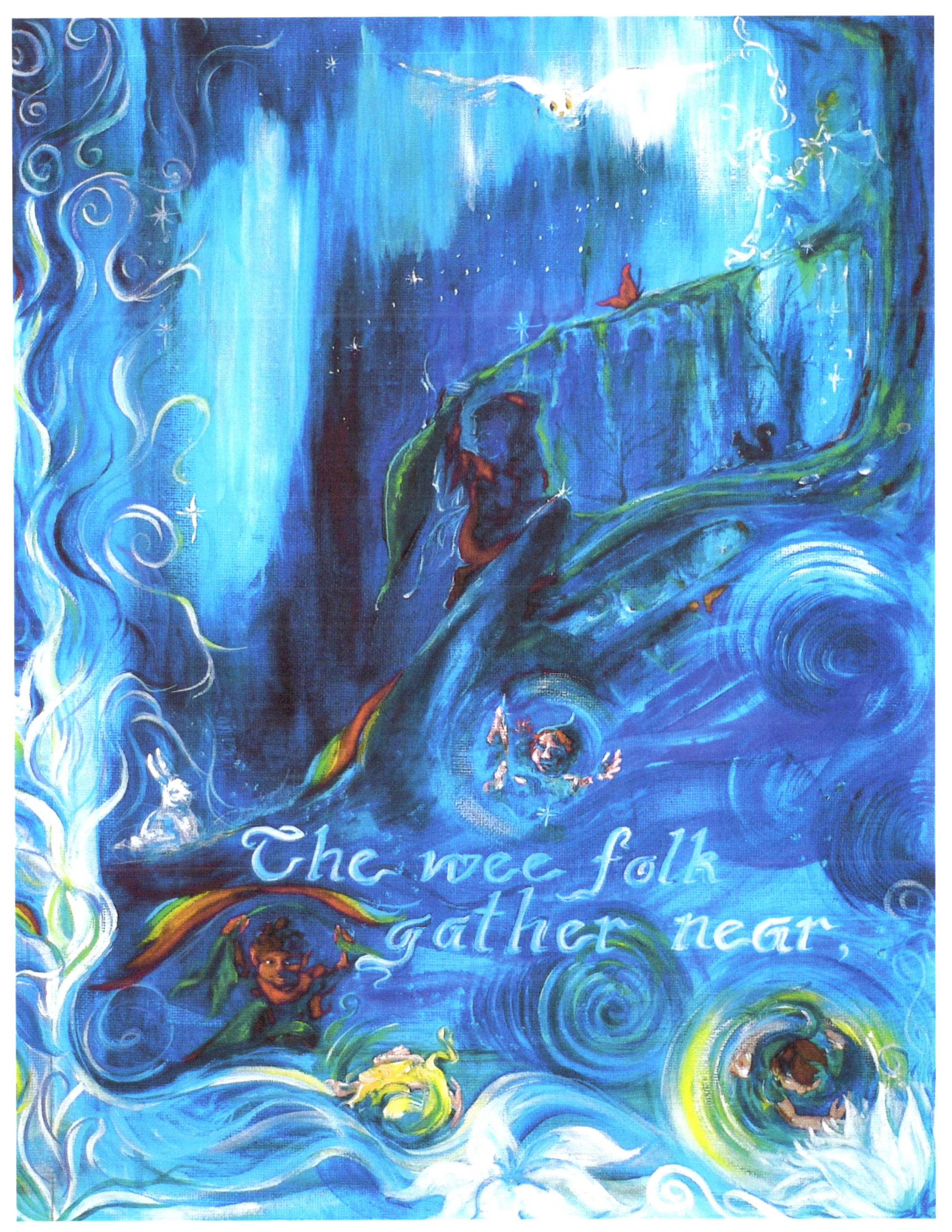


*The wee folk gather near,*

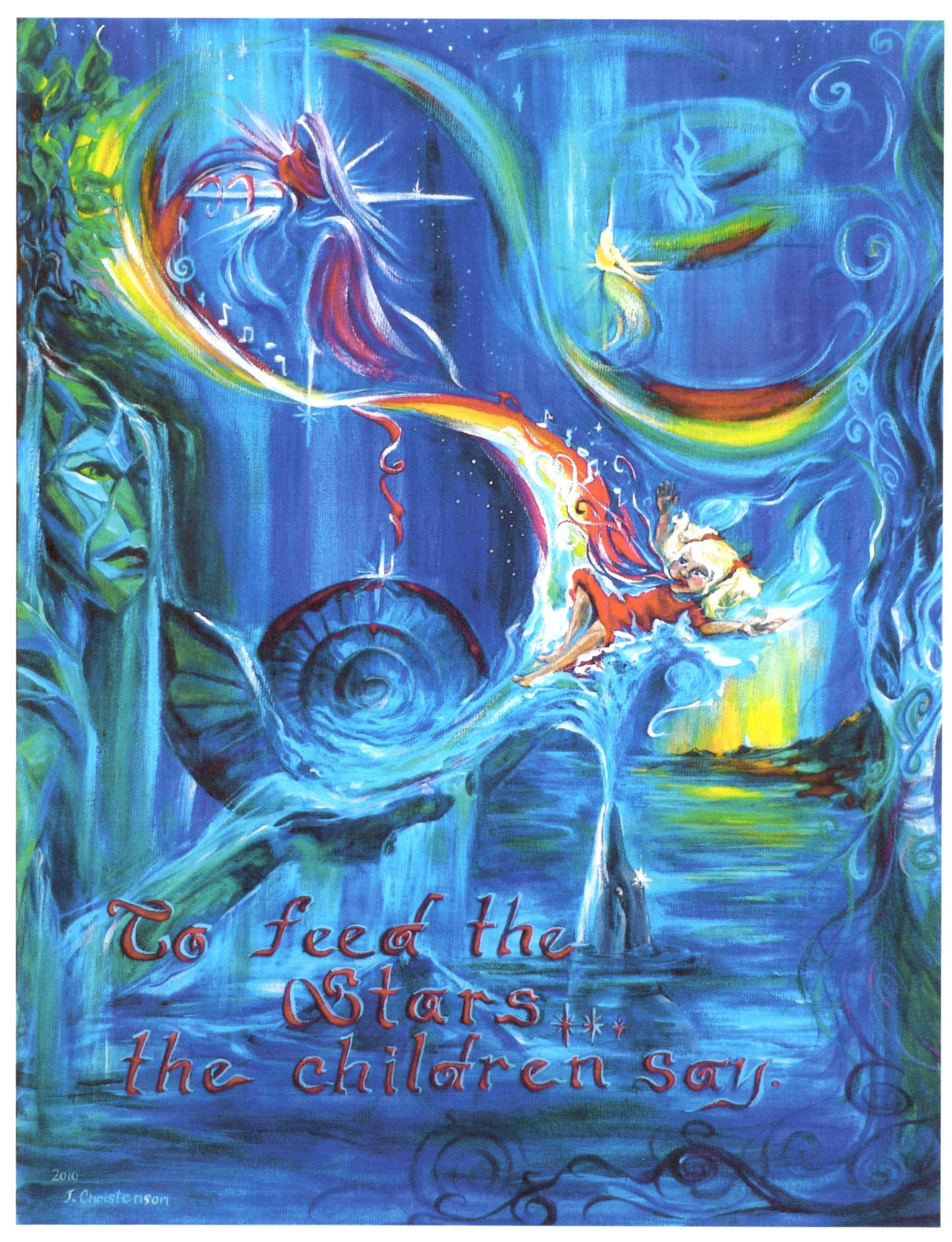


*To feed the stars the children say,*

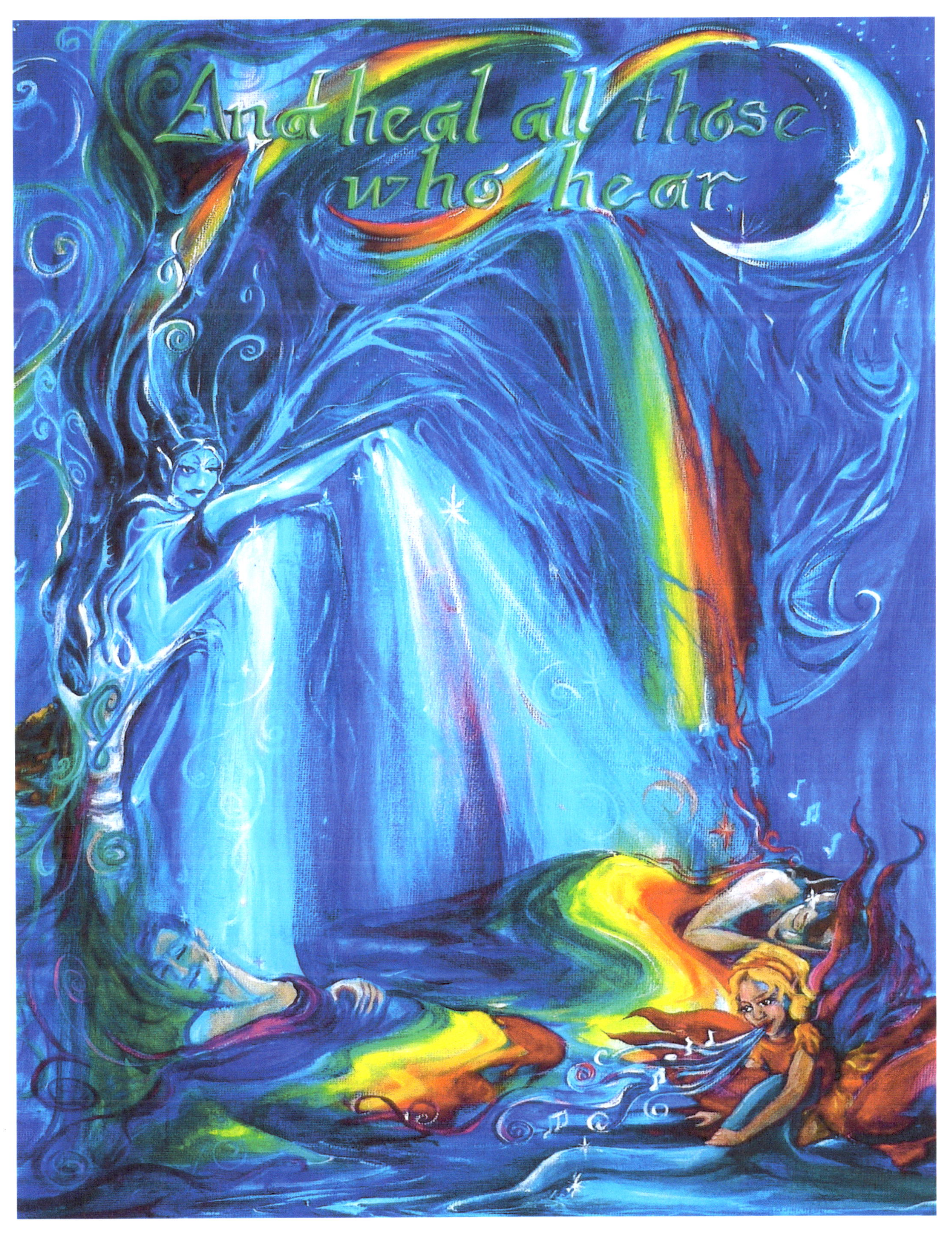


And heal all those who hear.

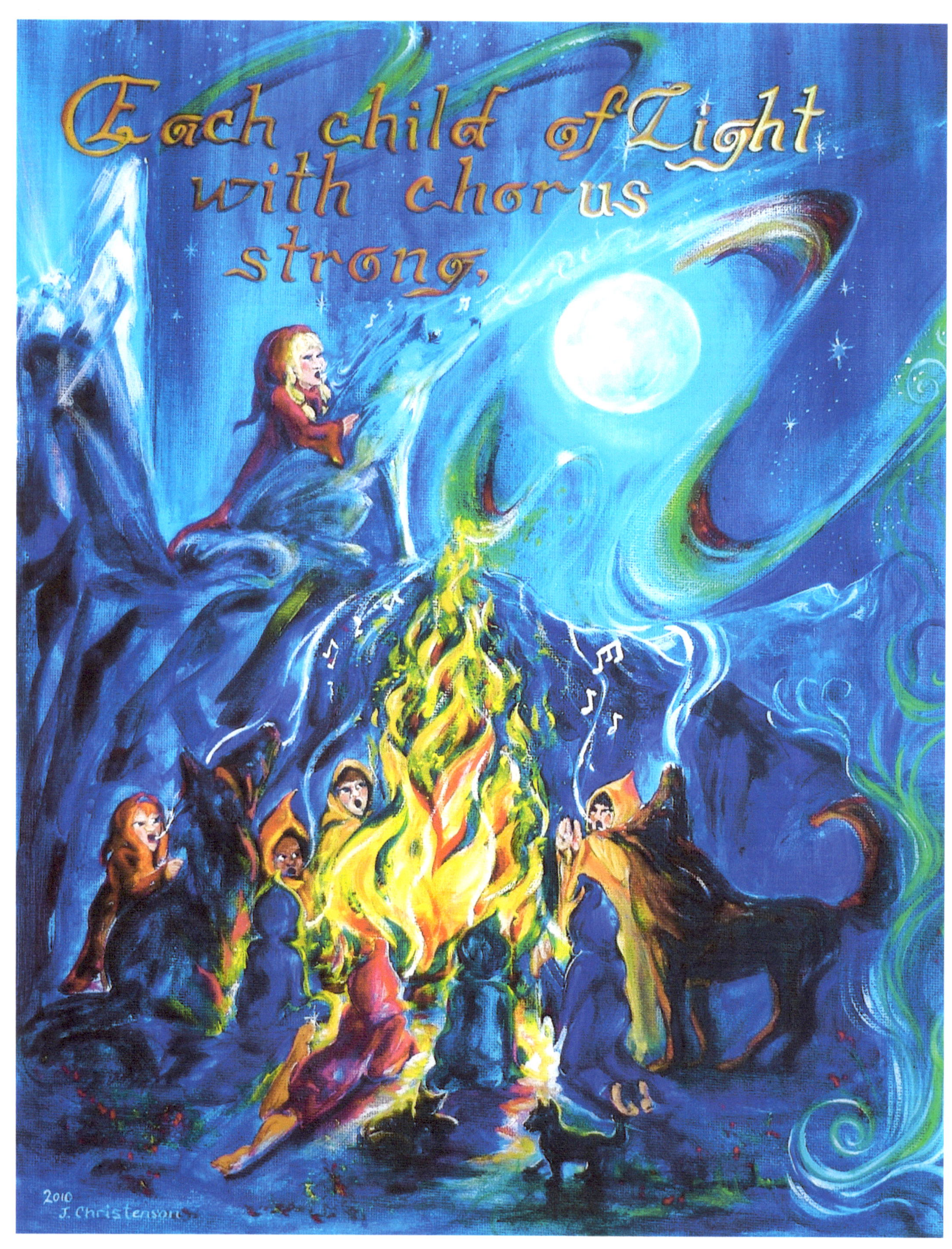


*Each child of light with chorus strong*

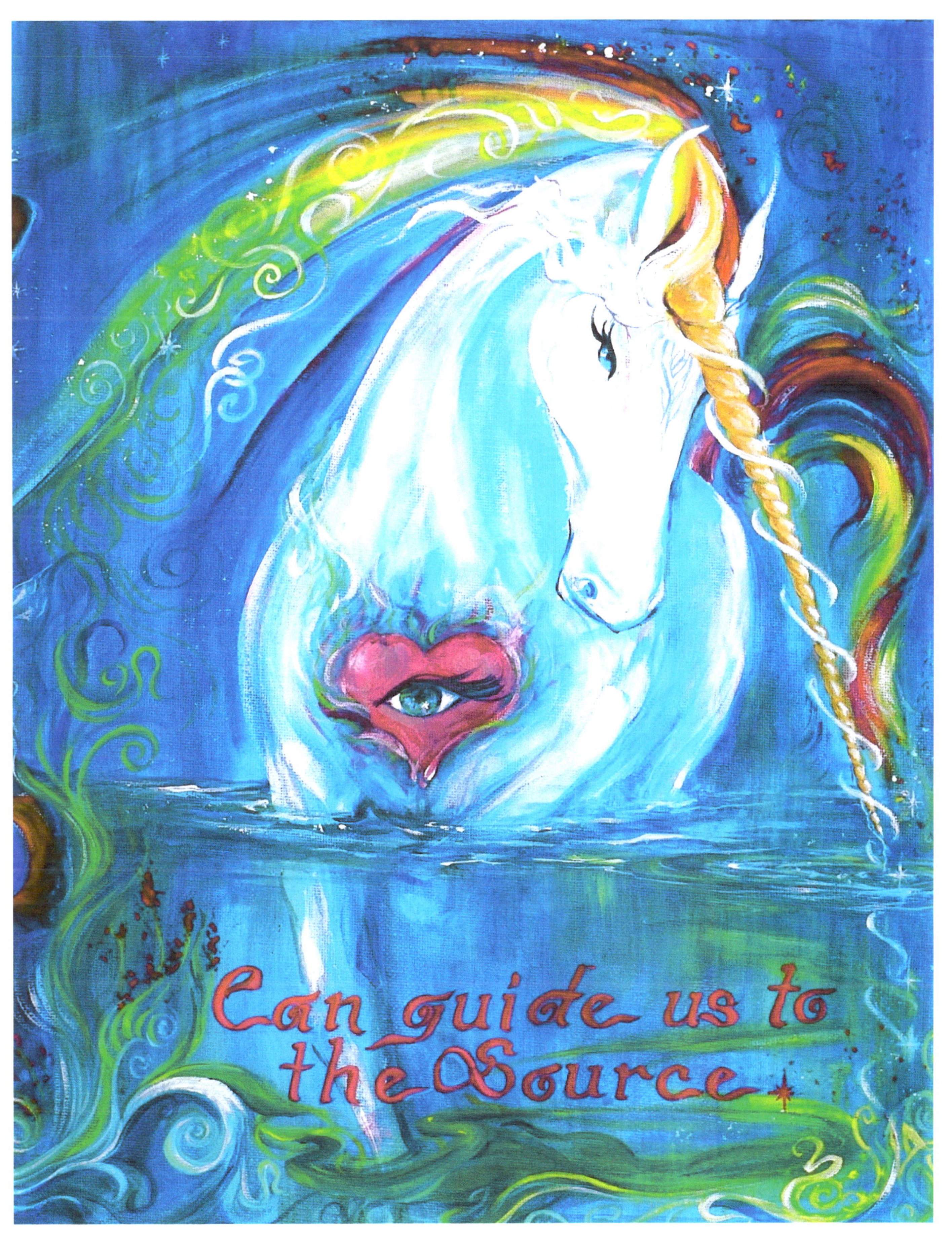


*Can guide us to the source,*

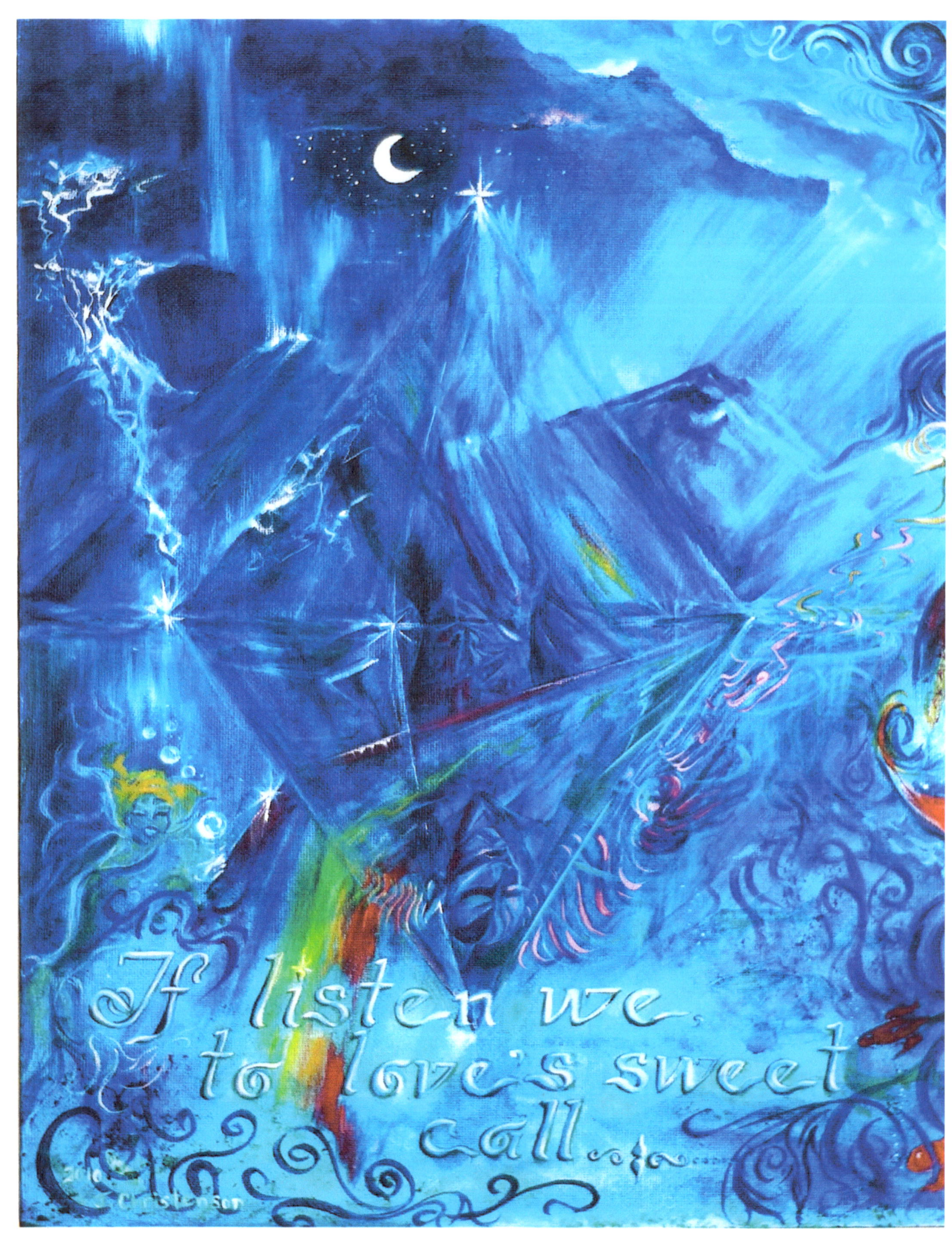


*If listen we to love's sweet call*

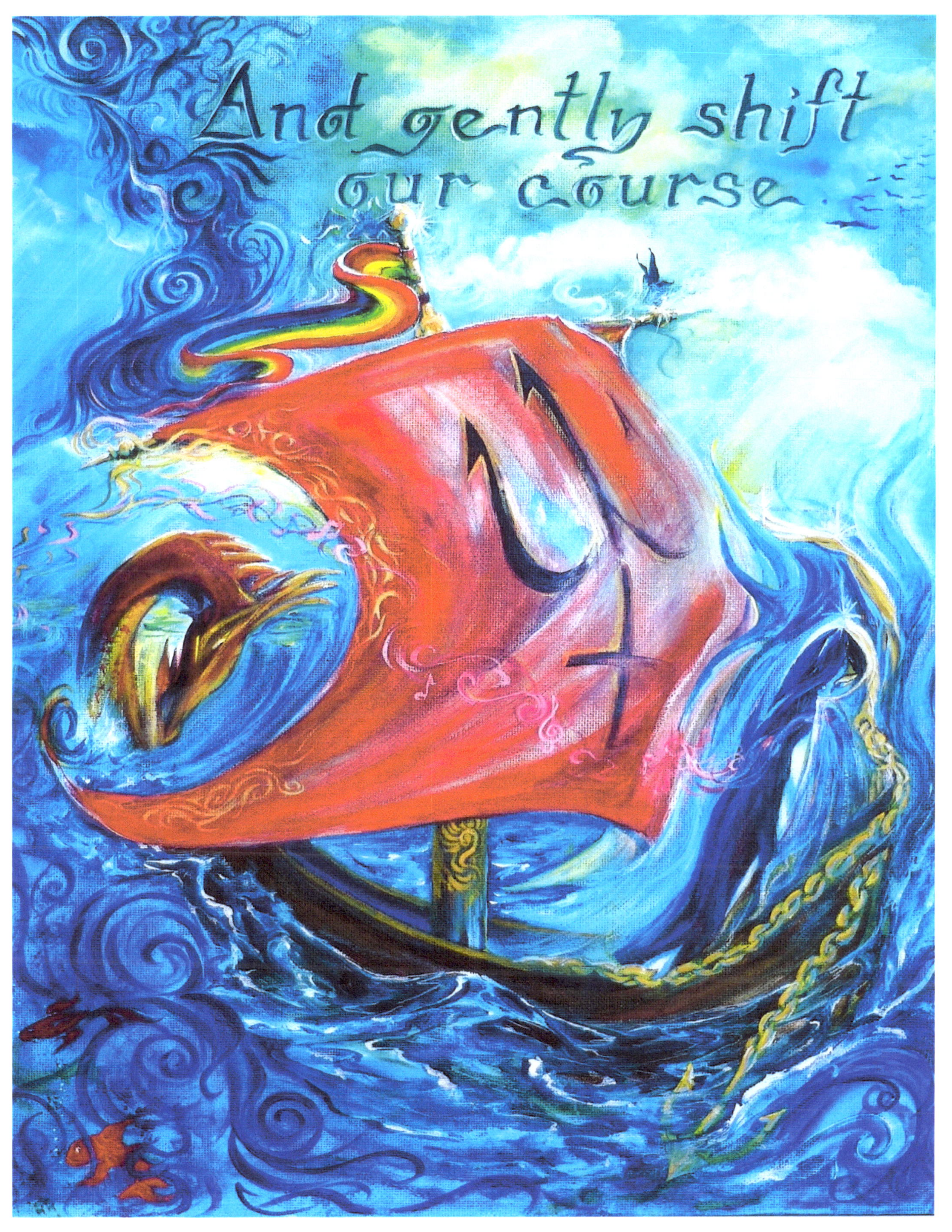


*And gently shift our course.*

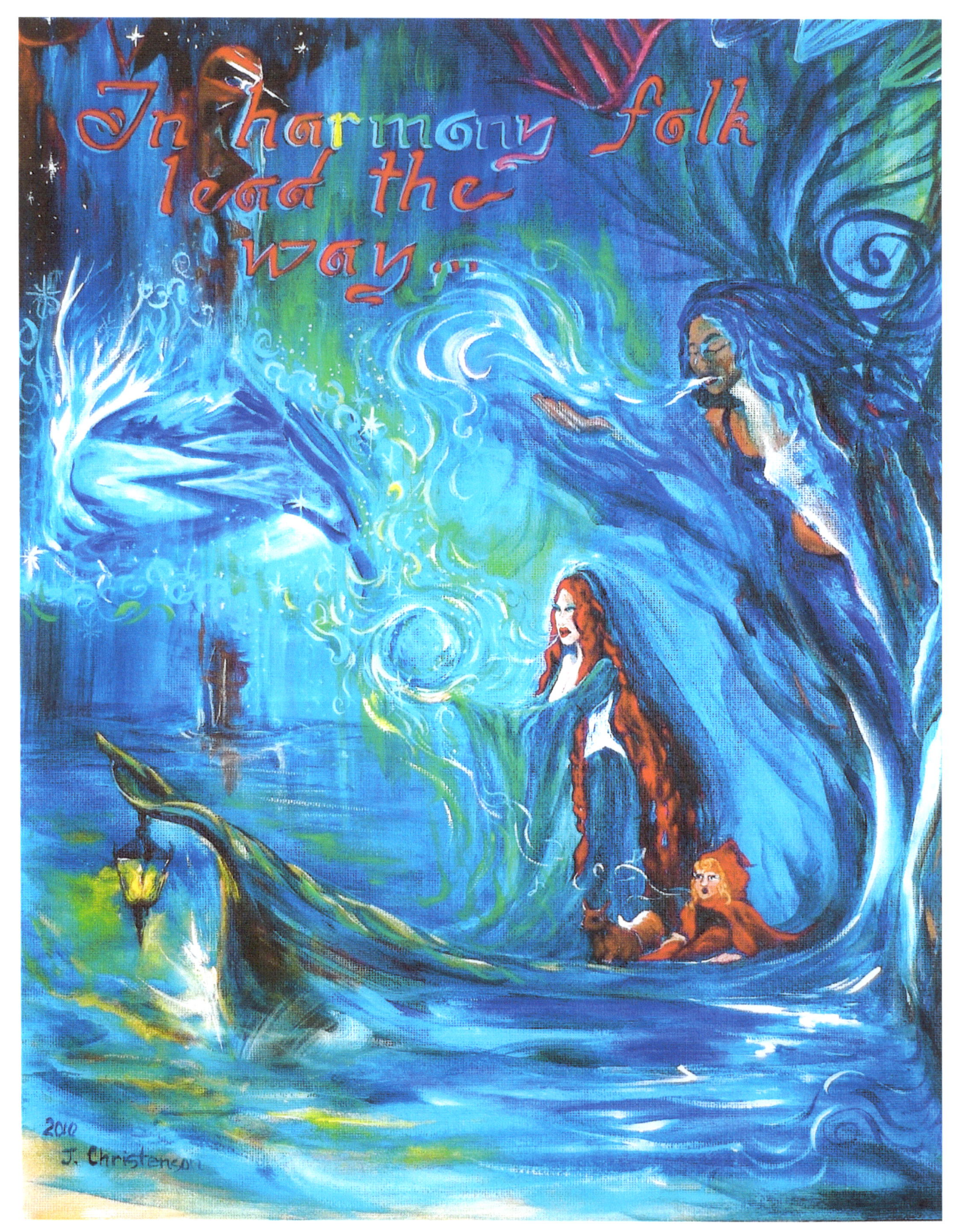


*In harmony folk lead the way...*

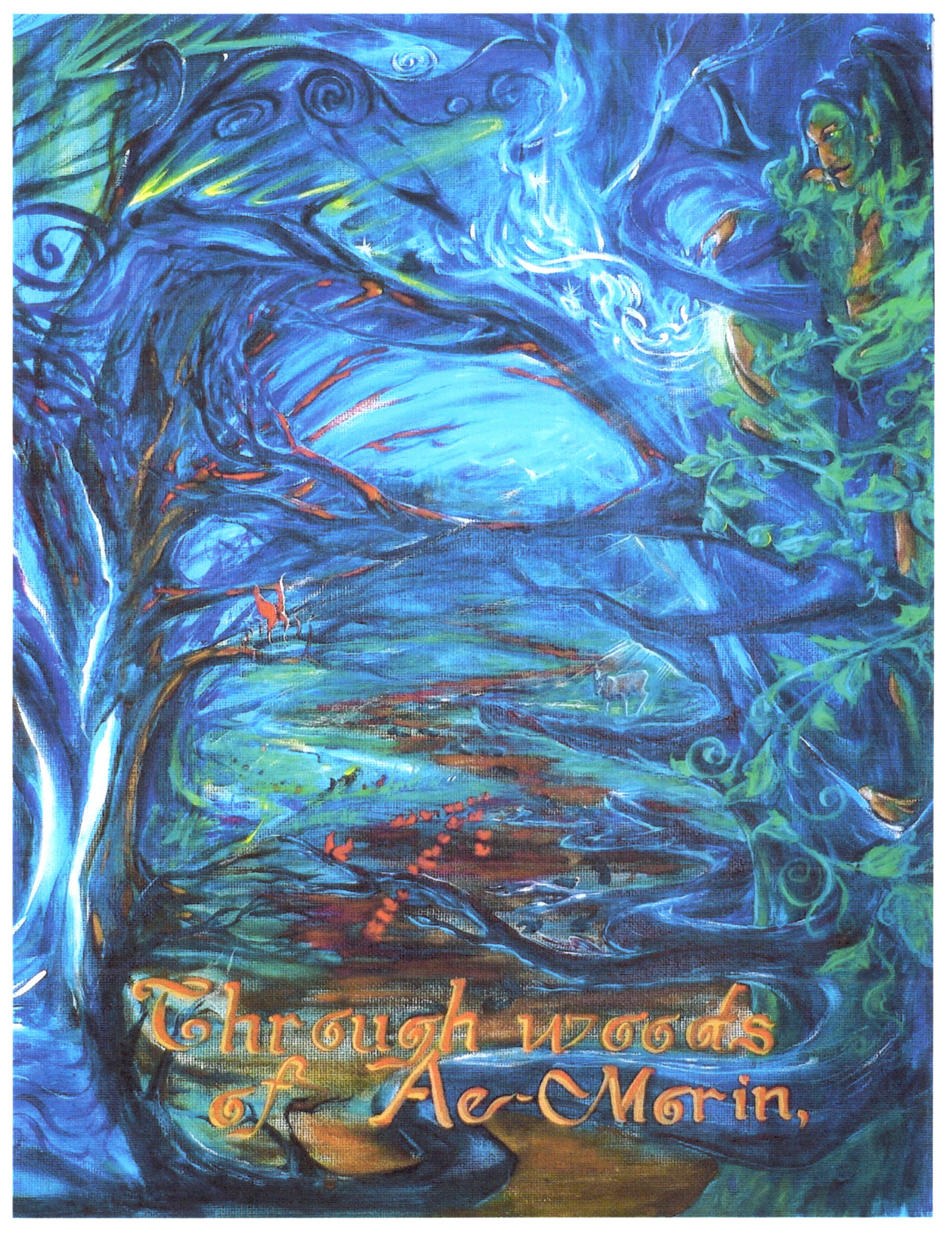


*Through woods of Ae-Morin,*

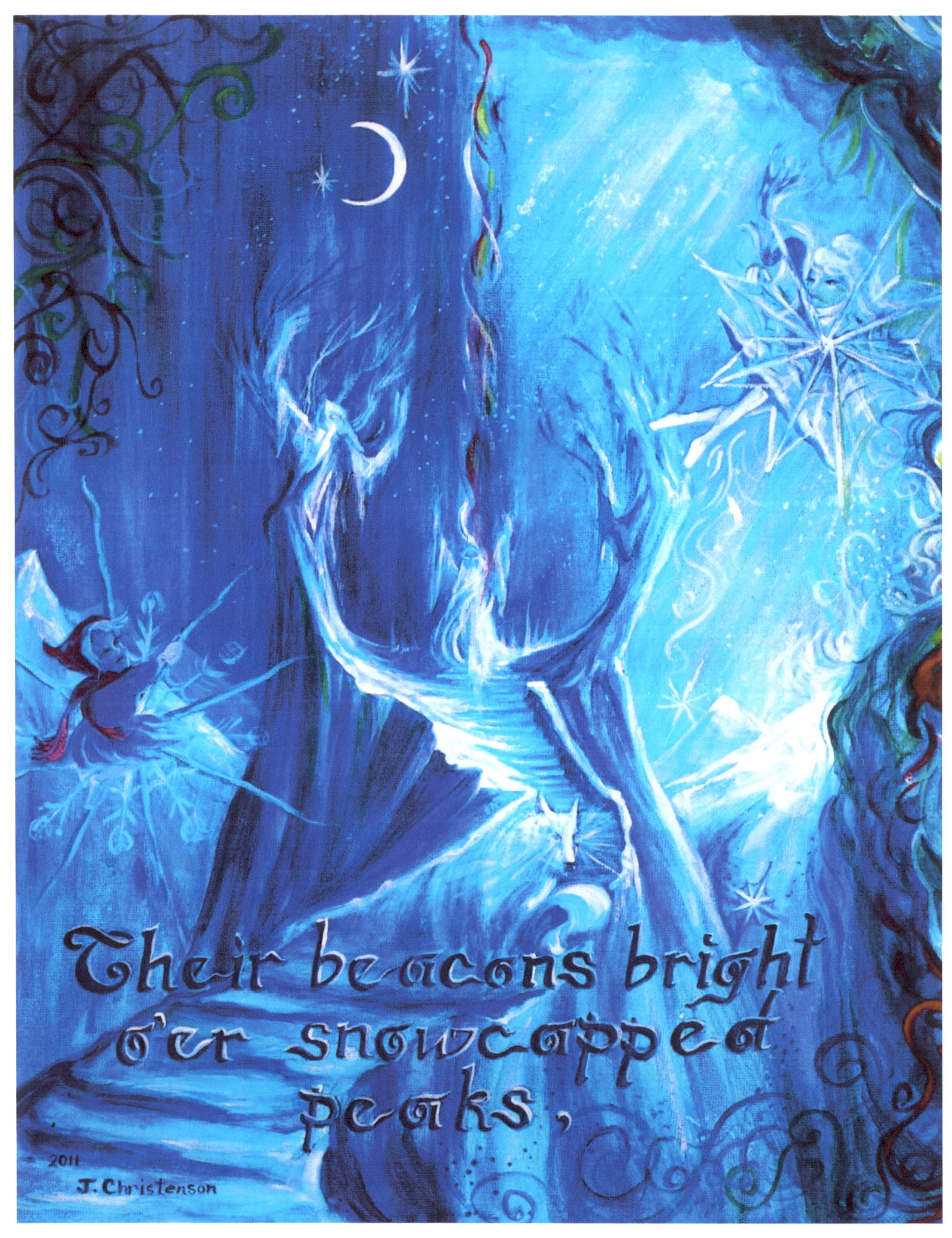


*Their beacon's bright o'er snowcapped Peaks,*

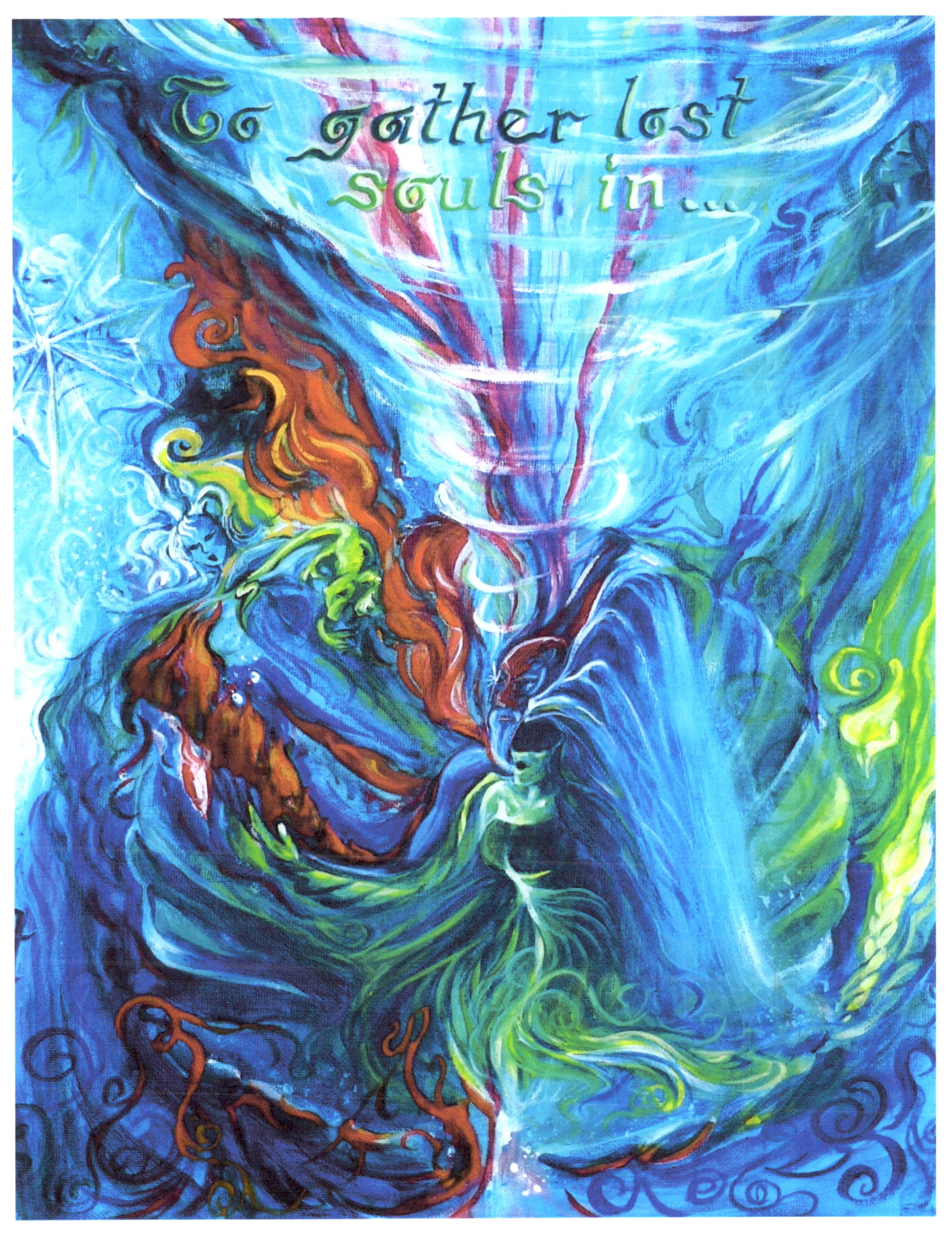


to gather lost souls in...

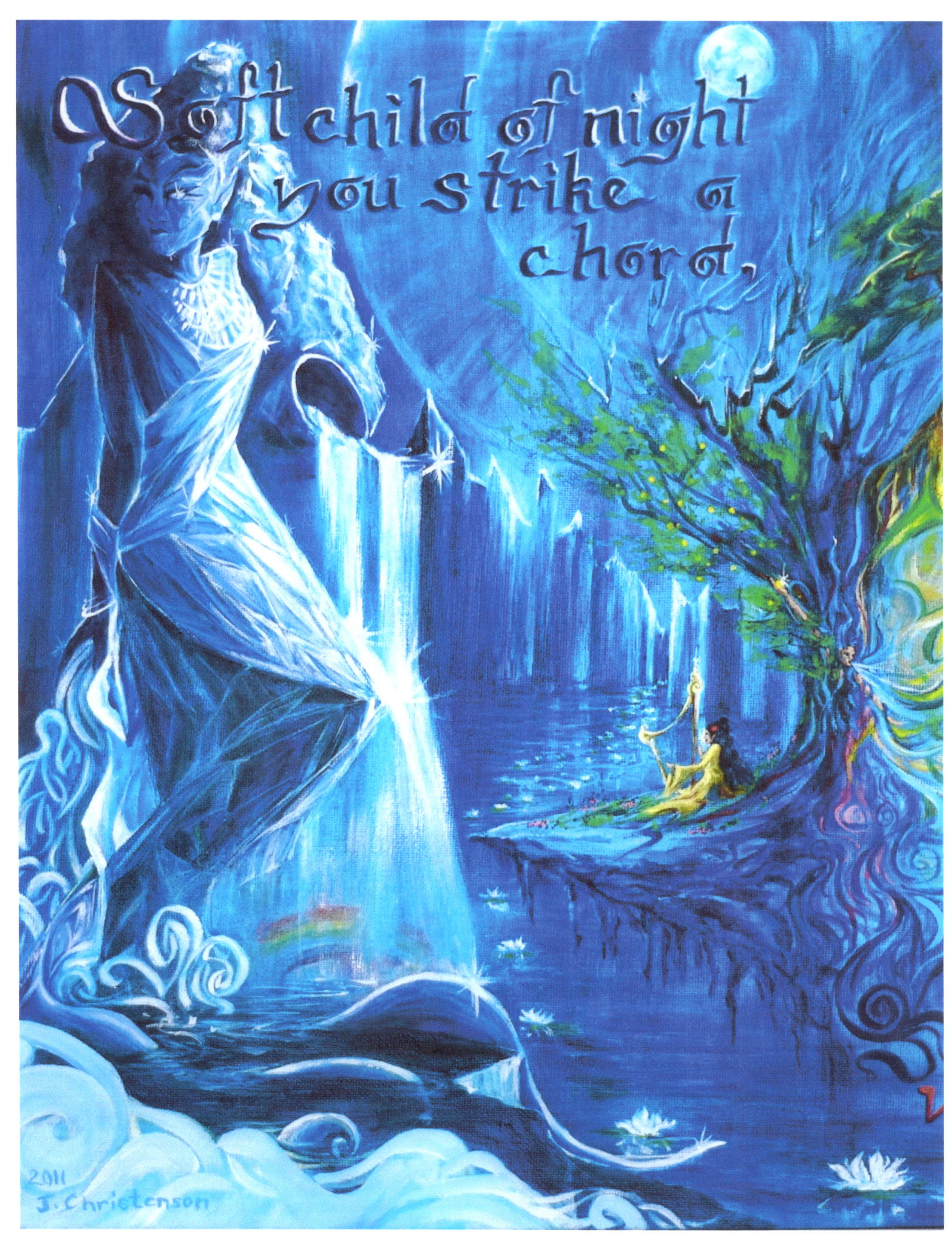


*Soft child of night you strike a chord,*

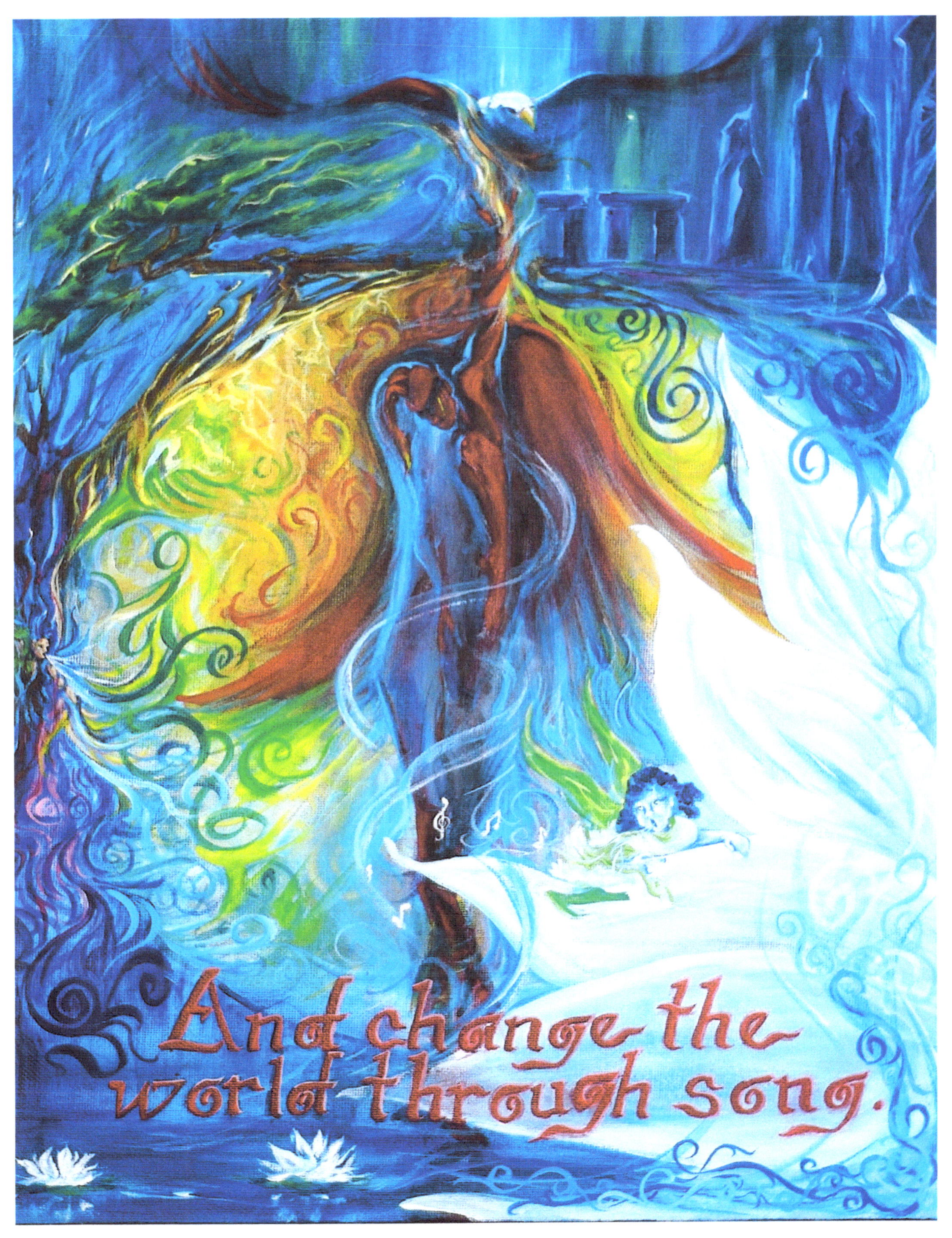


*And change the world through song.*

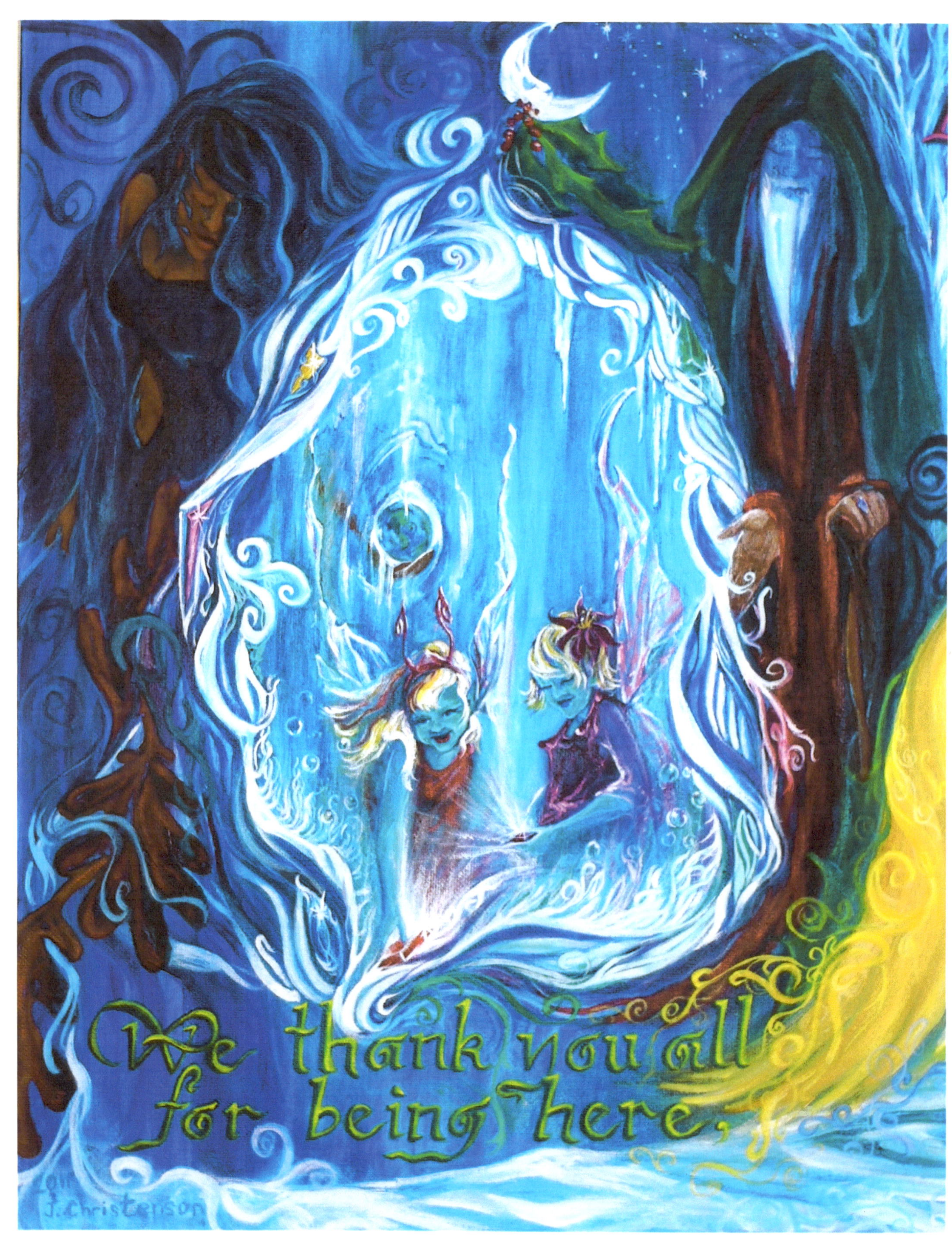


*We thank you all for being here,*

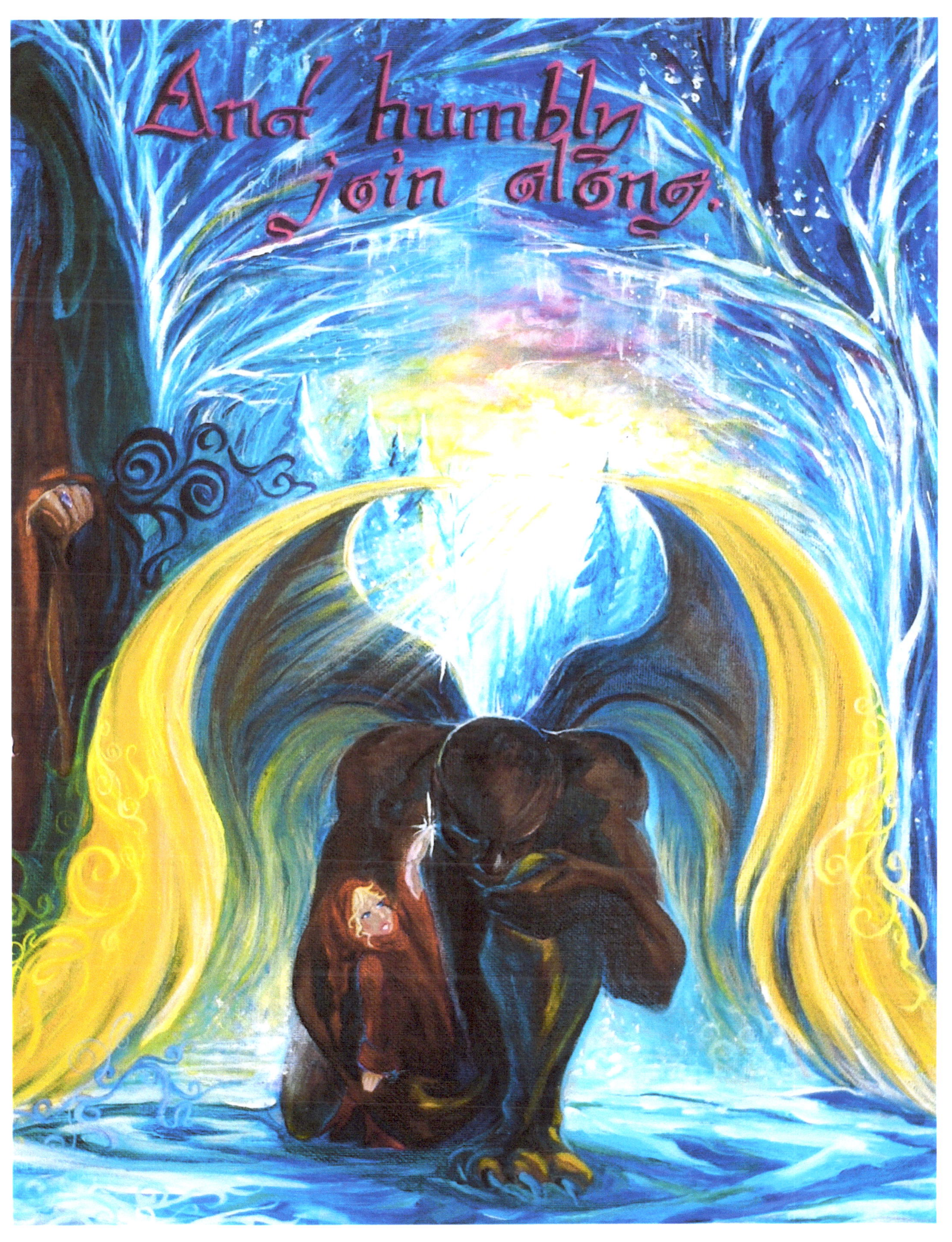


*And humbly join along.*

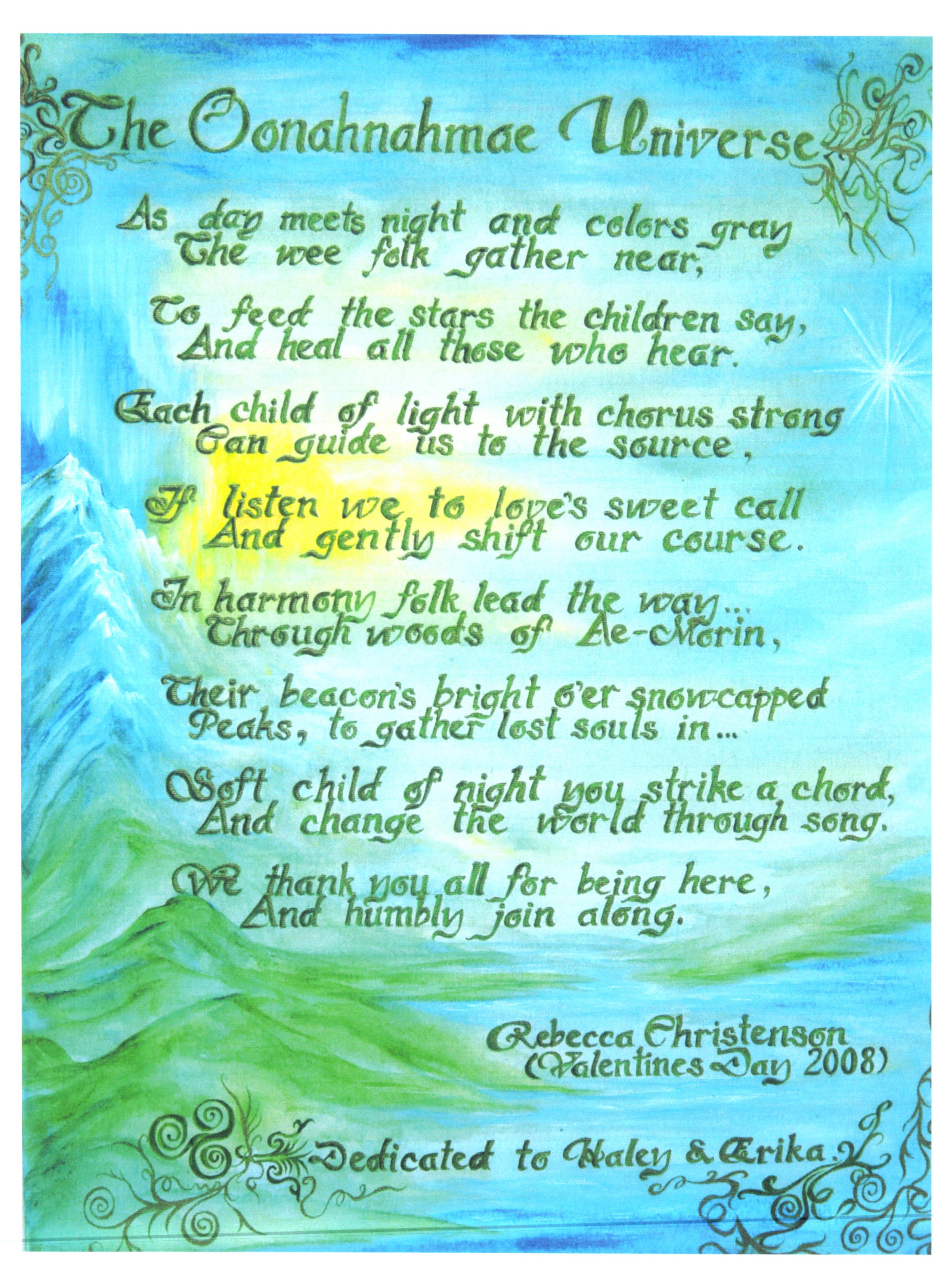
The Oonahnahmae Universe
As day meets night and colors gray
The wee folk gather near,
To feed the stars the children say,
And heal all those who hear.
Each child of light with chorus strong
Can guide us to the source,
If listen we to love's sweet call
And gently shift our course.
In harmony folk lead the way...
Through woods of Ae-Morin,
Their beacon's bright o'er snowcapped
Peaks, to gather lost souls in...
Soft child of night you strike a chord,
And change the world through song.
We thank you all for being here,
And humbly join along.
Rebecca Christenson
(Valentines Day 2008)
Dedicated to Haley & Erika.

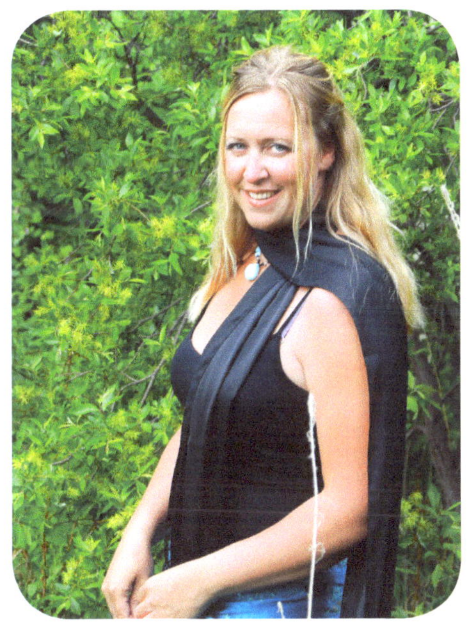

Rebecca Christenson is a mother, writer/producer, and work in progress. Her passion for visual expression motivated studies in; business, film production/screenwriting and communications at Lakeland College, SAIT Polytechnic, and Athabasca University, respectively.

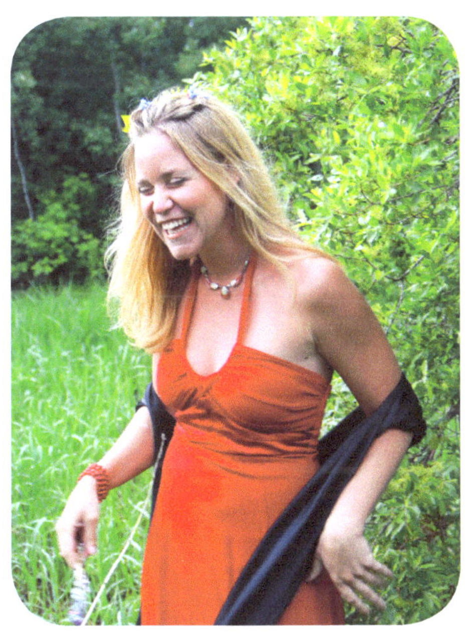

Jennifer Christenson is an aunty, fine artist, and work in progress. Her passion for visual arts motivated her studies in art and design, fine art, and costume design/construction at Red Deer College, Nova Scotia College of Art and Design, and Dalhousie University, respectively.

Both live in Alberta, Canada.

You are invited to: www.aquarian-creations.ca.
The Oonahnahmae Universe prints are available at:
www.jennifer-christenson.artistwebsites.com.

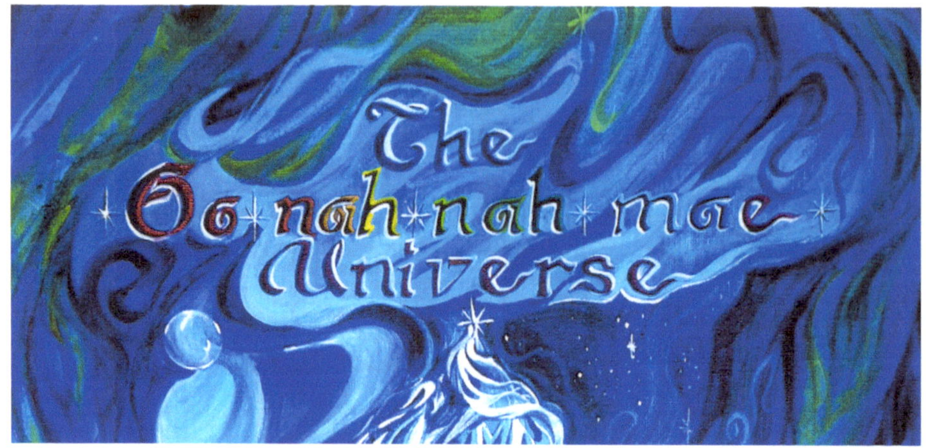


The Story behind the Poem (Song):

One evening, as I put my daughter to bed, she exclaimed, "Mommy! We didn't feed the stars their supper!"

I noted genuine concern, in this girl, who was only two and a half years old (at the time).

"Well," I responded, "What do the stars eat?"... Her earnest reply was:

"Stars eat songs."

She instructed me to open the blinds so we could see them. When I returned to sit beside her bed, I asked, "What should we sing?" In a tiny lilting voice, she began. It sounded Hawaiian, and was complete with a repeating chorus. "Sing with me, Mommy.", she urged.

I did my best to keep up, (in her language). Tears sprang to my eyes. The room was flooded in starlight, and deep peace blanketed us afterward.

"Oonahnahmae" is the only word I remember. Part of me wishes I would have dashed for a video camera or my journal to record more of the language, but I also knew the moment would have been lost.

As a life-long seeker, in that moment I experienced something different -- being "found". I thought about how easy it is to love children, and everyone is someone's child.

Almost a year later, I was feeling melancholy on Valentine's Day. My kids were at their Dad's, and shared parenting was a challenge (my heart literally hurt). Love is never limited by geography, so the solution was...find the space of love. I returned to that bedroom, on that night, and found the peace I sought.

I wrote for my children, and unbeknownst to me, my younger self. I have always found solace through creation, but in that moment it became a conscious choice for peace.

"The Oo*nah*nah*mae Universe" became my mantra, reminding me to; create, honor stillness, love the child within everyone, and work with reverent humility.

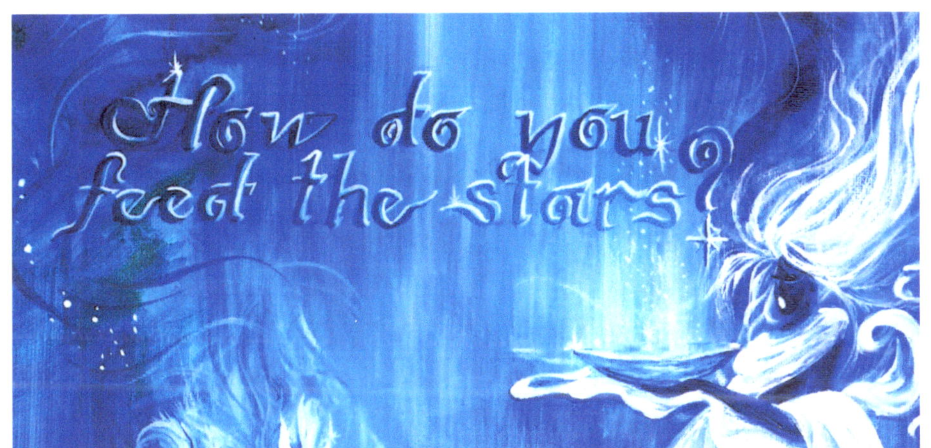


The Story behind the Paintings:

Jennifer Christenson painted The Oonahnahmae Universe the first time in 2008. It was originally exhibited during "Ostara: A Freedom Festival", the second Aquarian art show.

Afterwards, the canvas was hung in Jennifer's niece's bedroom and became part of their evening routine. One night, Jen heard the girls' voices (over the phone) and was compelled to paint it out again, this time line by line, panel by panel.

Jen layers information in minute detail engaging her viewers. In each panel, she worked to capture the singsong flow of the poem, moving left to right, up and down. It pays homage to cyclical nature and the restorative properties of night.

Jen's nieces have treasure hunted through these images for: musical notes, rainbows, magical creatures, and sources of light. This is the book she would have loved to see as a child. The Oonahnahmac dreamscapes, with feminine aspects intact, are balanced and thriving.

Feeding the stars is about getting to the place in life where you fill yourself up, from the inside. Then, at a certain point, your "bowl of light" becomes so bright it inevitably spills out into all that is.

This piece continues to give back to us in ways we couldn't have imagined. It is an ongoing work of heart.

So...How do you feed the stars?

*The Oonahnahmae Project*

*Star of Gold,*
*Star of Red,*
*Awaken together,*
*Through song we are fed.*

*Hearts for truth,*
*Rise above,*
*Resounding freedom in*
*A story of Love.*

*Written by: Jennifer Christenson*

www.ingramcontent.com/pod-product-compliance
Lightning Source LLC
LaVergne TN
LVHW070208110826
845147LV00002B/535

*9781426965012*